Simply Read the Basics, or
really Discover the Details!

Grand Canyon Rim to Rim

A Baby Ranger Book

Written,Illustrated & Published by:
Briana Owens

babyrangerbooks.com

Copyright © 2021

Are you ready to hike RIM to RIM at the Grand Canyon?

First thing to do: Study the map!

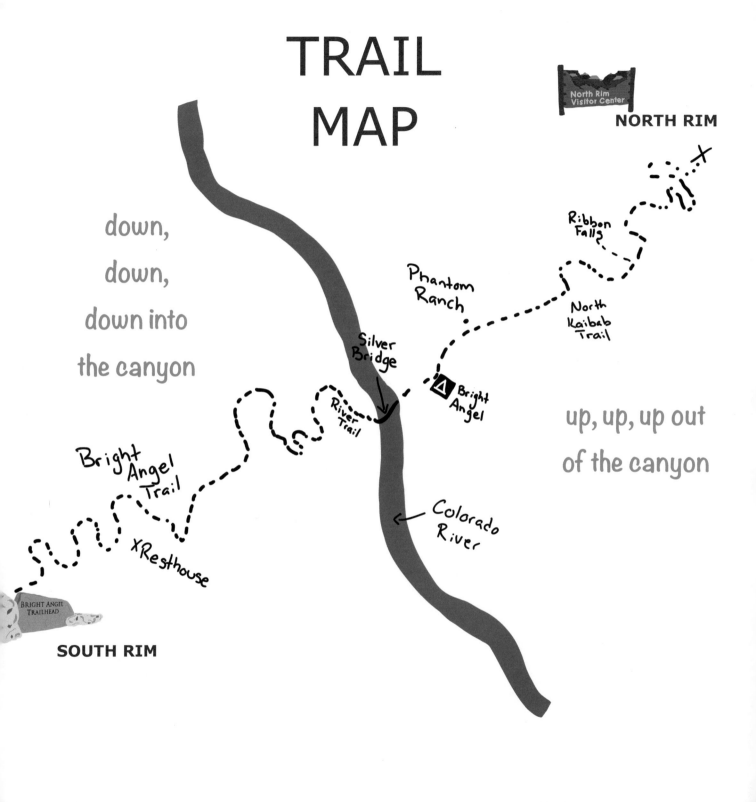

Second: pack properly, and be prepared!

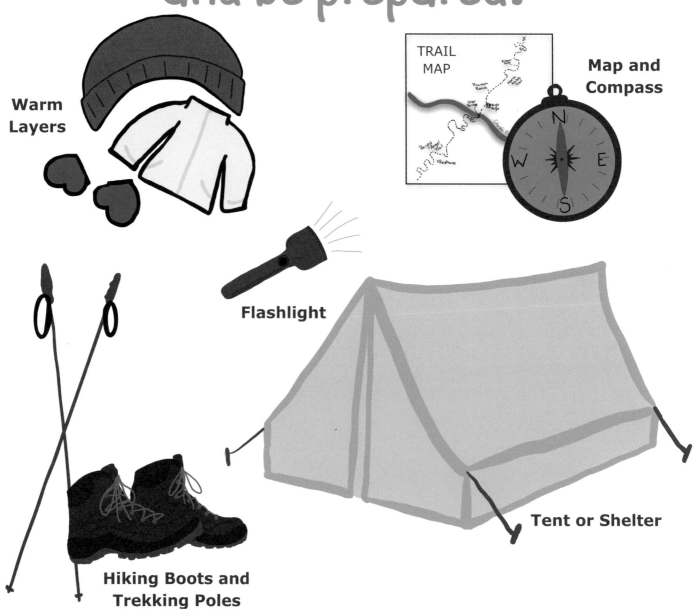

Warm Layers

Map and Compass

TRAIL MAP

Flashlight

Tent or Shelter

Hiking Boots and Trekking Poles

First Aid Kit

Food and Water

Hat and Sunglasses

Safety Whistle

Prepare by reading books about the Grand Canyon

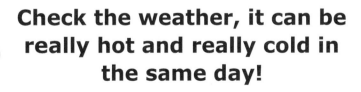

Check the weather, it can be really hot and really cold in the same day!

Third: make sure all water bottles are filled.

Let the ADVENTURE begin!

Baby Ranger sees:

plants and animals

Abert's Squirrel

Pinyon Pine

Asters

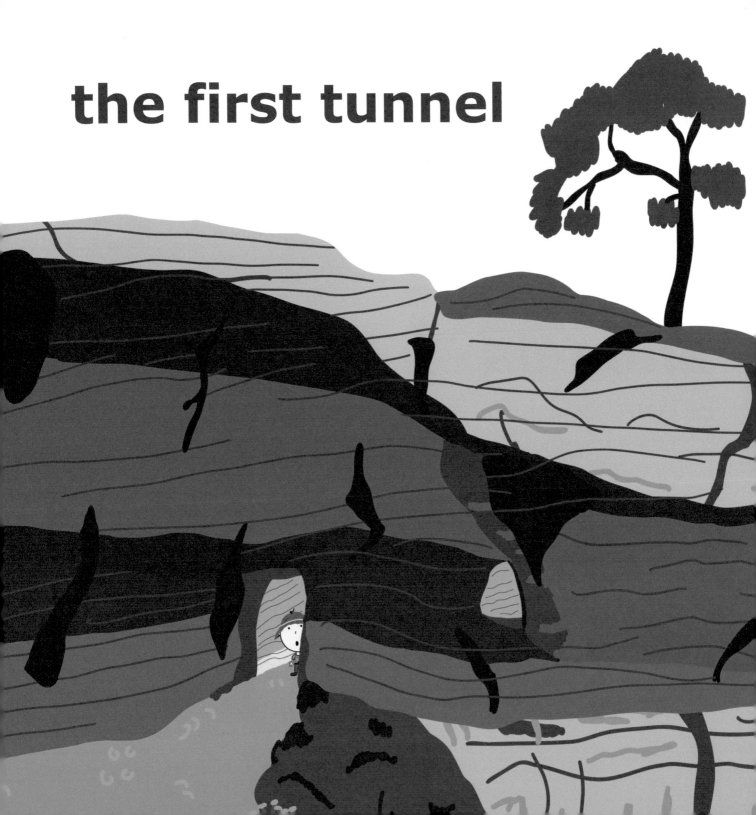

the first tunnel

pictographs

These are paintings on the rock from a long, long time ago!

and a mule!

When mules pass
Stand to the inside of trail
Follow mule guides instructions

Some people choose to tour the Grand Canyon by riding mules!

Baby Ranger sees:
more plants

Globe Mallow

Douglas Fir

Banana Yucca

Prickly Pear

a rest-house

Time for snacks!

and more rock art!

Baby Ranger sees a snake, a frog and footprints... what do you see?

Baby Ranger sees:
the Silver Bridge

BRIGHT ANGEL CAMP
PHANTOM RANCH

← BRIGHT ANGEL TRAIL

S. KAIBAB TRAIL →

lizards and a rattlesnake

**Yellow-backed
Spiny Lizard**

Common Earless Lizard

Grand Canyon Pink Rattlesnake
Lives only at the Grand Canyon!

rafts on the Colorado River

Some people choose to tour the Grand Canyon by rafting on the river!

and Bright Angel Campground!

Baby Ranger sees:

bats

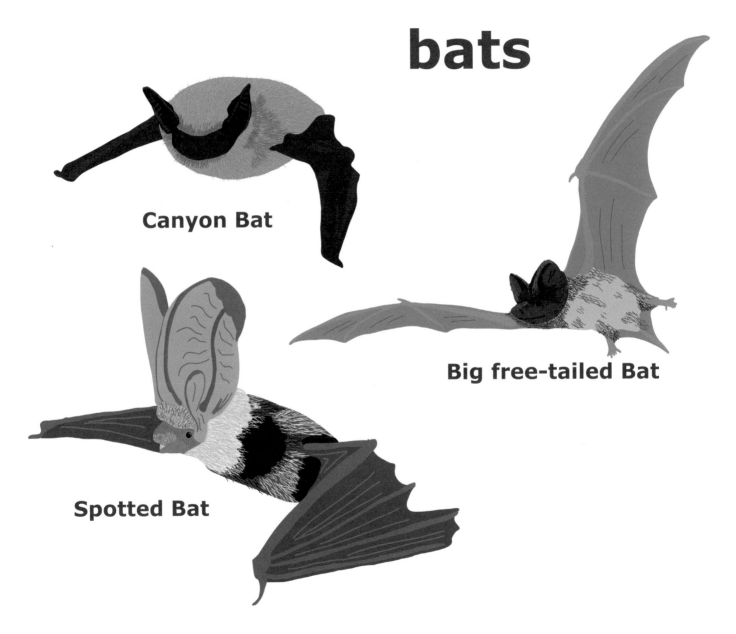

Canyon Bat

Big free-tailed Bat

Spotted Bat

butterflies

Kaibab Swallowtail

Anise Swallowtail

Variegated Fritillary

and Phantom Ranch

Known as a "historic oasis" below the canyon rim. There are dorms and cabins for people to stay in, and a canteen where they can eat.

PHANTOM RANCH WELCOMES YOU

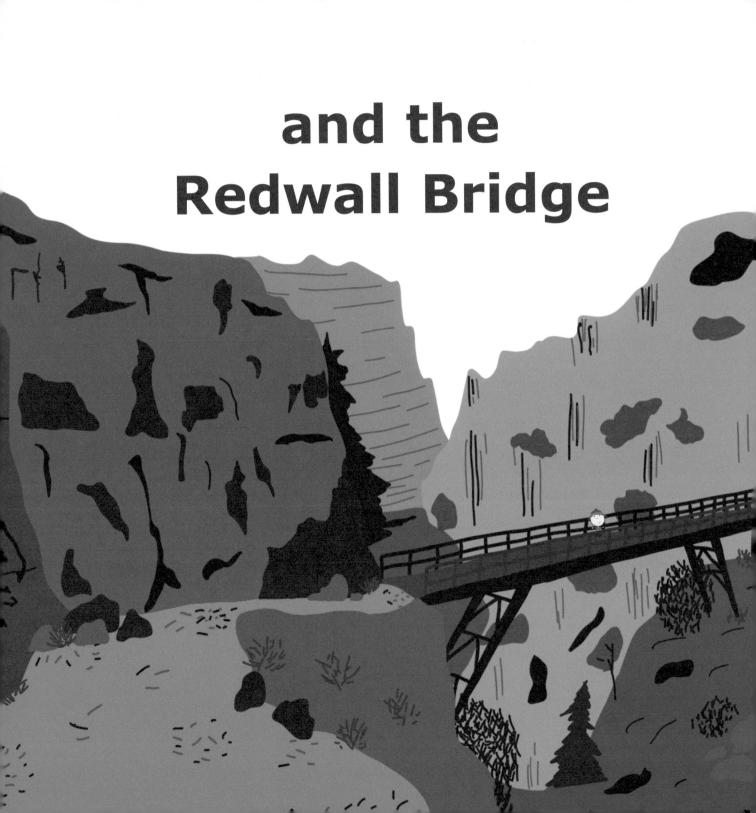

Almost to the top!

Hiking

UP, UP, UP

is a lot of

work!

It's the Supai Tunnel!

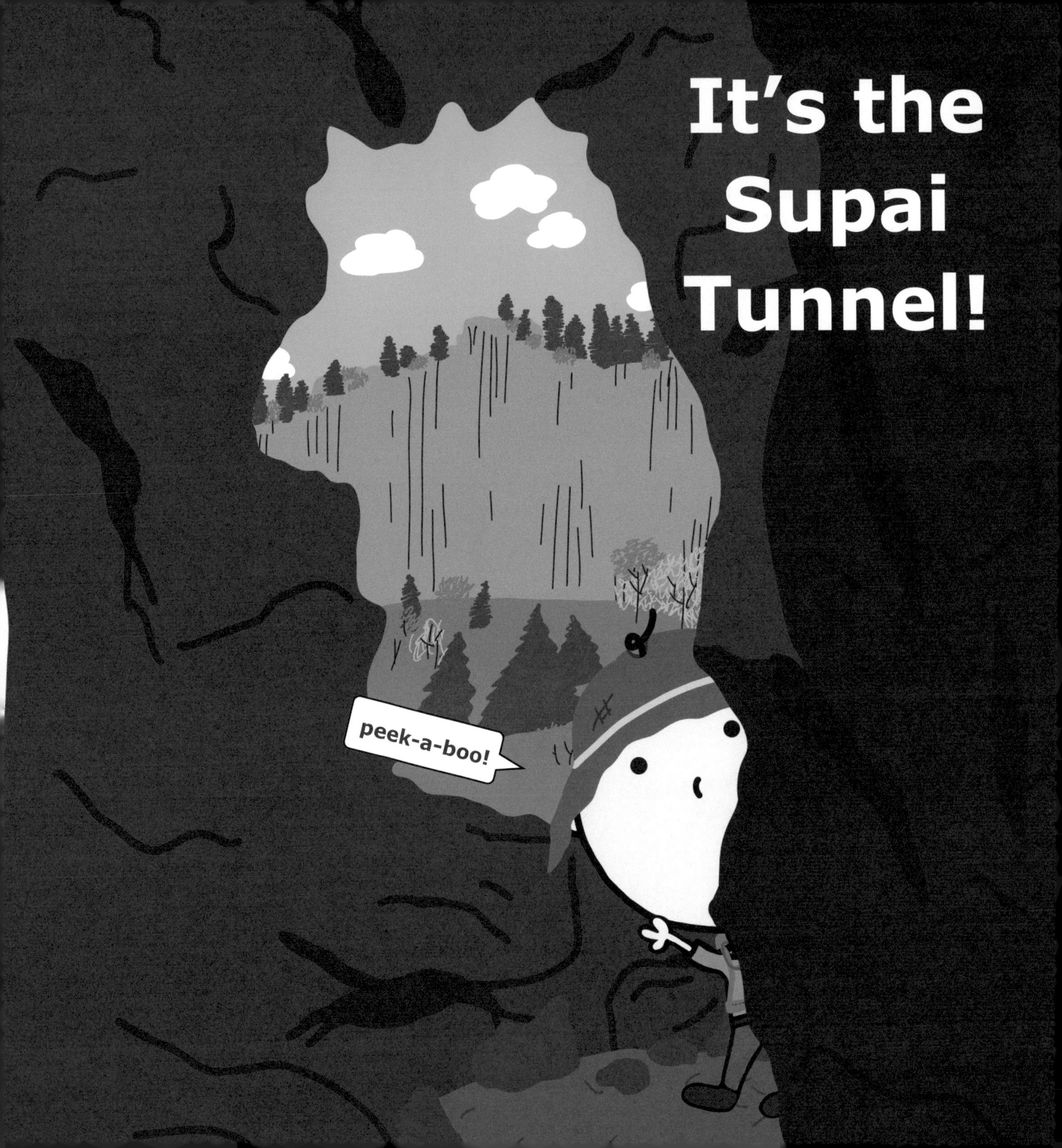

WE MADE IT!!!

to RIM

at the
Grand Canyon!

Made in the USA
Columbia, SC
06 December 2023